THE FOREST THROUGH THE TREES

Jason Pitts

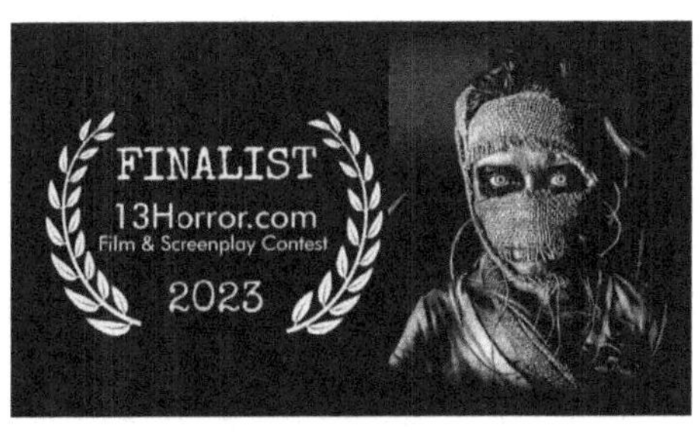

13HORROR.COM BOOKS
An imprint of
DIZZY EMU PUBLISHING
1714 N McCadden Place, Hollywood, Los Angeles 90028
dizzyemupublishing.com

The Forest Through The Trees
Jason Pitts

First published in the United States
in 2023 by 13Horror.com Books/Dizzy Emu Publishing

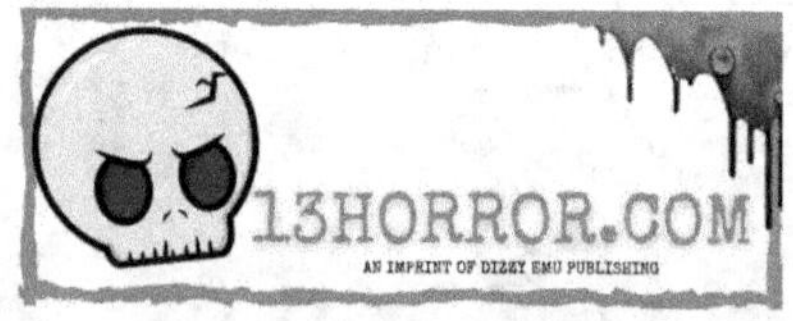

THE FOREST THROUGH THE TREES

Jason Pitts

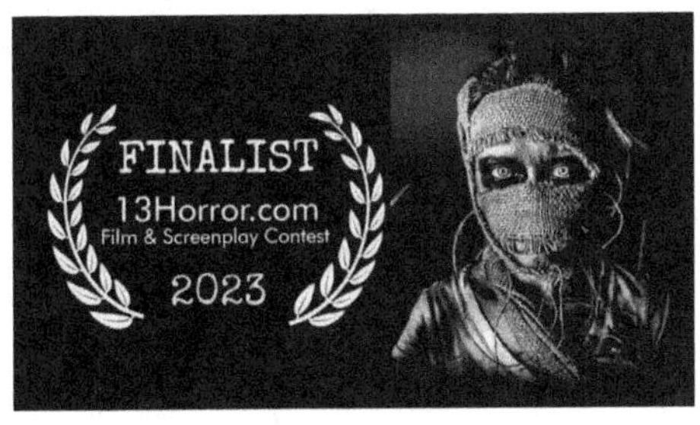

                                                     FADE IN:

EXT. WOODS - NIGHT

Trees sway in the breeze. The forest conceals it's
secrets in a shroud of darkness. SCREAMS can be heard, as
we see a cabin.

INT. CABIN BEDROOM - NIGHT

KATHY, late teens/early 20's, is in labor. Her sister,
RUTH, late teens/early 20's, is helps her deliver the
baby.

                         RUTH
               Push! Kathy, you're almost there!
               Push!

Kathy screams as she pushes. The CRIES of a baby fill the
room. Ruth smiles as she wraps the newborn.

                         RUTH
               It's a girl!

Kathy smiles weakly, and reaches out to her daughter.

                         KATHY
               Let me hold my daughter.

Ruth hands the baby to Kathy. Kathy looks down at her
daughter's face. The baby opens her eyes, revealing one
blue eye and one brown.

The color drains from Kathy's face, as she panics.

                         KATHY
               No, no, no. Please, no.

Ruth sees the baby's eyes and GASPS, hands to her mouth.

                         RUTH
               I'll get the elders.

                         KATHY
               No! Wait!

They stare at each other, while the baby cries.

                         KATHY
               I can take her away.

                                              (CONTINUED)

CONTINUED:

                              RUTH
                    This is what everyone has been
                    waiting for.

                              KATHY
                    They'll kill her! Ruth, you're my
                    sister. Help me. Please. We can
                    just disappear, the 3 of us.

Ruth takes a moment to think. She turns her back on her
sister and looks out the window of the cabin.

                              KATHY
                    Ruthie? Please!

Ruth shakes her head.

                              RUTH
                    No. I can't leave.

                              KATHY
                    Then let us go.

                              RUTH
                    What would I tell him?

                              KATHY
                    I don't know. Tell him the baby
                    died, and I was so ashamed I ran.

Ruth closes her eyes, a tear runs down her cheek. She
takes a deep breath.

                              RUTH
                    Okay, but I'm staying.

Kathy looks down at her daughter again. The baby smiles
up at her with one blue eye and one brown eye.

INT. WILLIAMS' HOUSE - LIVING ROOM - NIGHT

CHLOE WILLIAMS, 19, one blue eye and one brown eye, TYPES
on a computer in a middle class living room.

The front door bursts open, and Kathy, 19 years older,
and KEN WILLIAMS, early 50's, muscular, enters the house.
They laugh as Ken closes the door behind them. Chloe
looks up and smiles at them.

                              CHLOE
                    Sounds like you love birds had a
                    great time!

                                                    (CONTINUED)

CONTINUED:

                    KATHY
          This guy doesn't know how to keep
          his hands to himself!

Ken pulls her close and kisses her.

                    KEN
          I can't resist.

Kathy tosses her keys on a table. Chloe resumes typing.

                    KATHY
          What are you still doing up? It's
          2 am?

Chloe keeps working.

                    CHLOE
          I'm a victim of procrastination.
          It's due today.

Kathy chuckles.

                    KATHY
          What have I taught you about not
          waiting to get your work done.

                    CHLOE
          Not helping!

                    KEN
          I'm going to take shower, hun.
          Come with me, and let's finish the
          night off right!

                    CHLOE
          Gross.

Kathy laughs.

                    KATHY
          I'll be there in just a minute.

Ken blows Kathy a kiss then exits down the hall. Kathy
watches him with a big smile on her face.

                    KATHY
          Cloe, we really got lucky when we
          met your dad.

                    CHLOE
          I guess...<u>Ken</u> is alright..

CONTINUED: (2)

                    KATHY
          I wish you wouldn't do that. He's
          as much as a father to you as
          anyone has been.

Chloe stops typing and turns to Kathy.

                    CHLOE
          You never talk about him.

                    KATHY
          And I'm not going to.

Chloe seethes at Kathy for a moment, then remembers...

                    CHLOE
          Someone left you some flowers. I
          put them on the table in the
          kitchen.

                    KATHY
          What?

Kathy walks into the kitchen.

INT. WILLIAMS' HOUSE - KITCHEN - CONTINUOUS

Kathy's eyes immediately fall on a vase of Marigold
flowers resting on the kitchen table.

Her eyes go wide in horror at the sight of the flowers.
She starts to hyperventilate.

                    KATHY
          Oh my god!

                    CHLOE (O.S.)
          Mom? Are you okay?

Kathy tries to compose herself.

                    KATHY
          I'm fine, dear. Did they see you?

                    CHLOE (O.S.)
          Who?

                    KATHY
          Whoever delivered these flowers?

                    CHLOE (O.S.)
          I didn't see anyone.

CONTINUED:

Kathy cautiously approaches the flowers. There is an envelope. She pulls out a small white index card. On one side it says, "Time to come home." She flips the card over. On the other side is a phone number. "555-2856".

Kathy quietly SOBS as she stares at the card.

INT. WILLIAMS' HOUSE - KEN'S BEDROOM - NIGHT

Kathy is frantically packing a small travel bag. The SHOWER can be heard from the bathroom. The door to the bathroom is slightly open, with a sliver of light cutting through the darkness of the bedroom.

                    KEN (O.S.)
          Babe? I hope you're stripping down
          for me!

Kathy zips up the bag, and scribbles down a note on a piece of paper. She places it on a nightstand. Kathy turns to the bathroom door.

                    KATHY
          I love you.

                    KEN (O.S.)
          What was that?

Kathy grabs her bag and walks out the door.

INT. WILLIAMS' HOUSE - LIVING ROOM - NIGHT

Chloe is typing. Kathy walks from the hallway into the kitchen behind her. Chloe stops typing, yawns, and rubs her eyes. She turns to look at the kitchen when she hears the back door CLOSE.

                    CHLOE
          Mom?

EXT. WILLIAM'S HOUSE - NIGHT

Kathy calls the number, as she hurries down the driveway.

                    KATHY
          I know you're watching. I'm ready.

She starts walking down the sidewalk, and puts her phone away. Kathy wipes away her tears as a black car pulls up next to her. The rear passenger side door opens, and Kathy gets in. The car drives off.

CONTINUED:

Ken, wrapped in a towel, hurries out the front door. He
looks up and down the street.

                    KEN
          Kathy?

EXT. SUBURBAN NEIGHBORHOOD - DAY

ONE YEAR LATER.

It is a beautiful sunny day. Chloe staples a missing
poster of Kathy to a telephone pole. AVA, early 20's with
a tattoo of a raven on her right shoulder, stands next to
her holding a stack of posters.

                    CHLOE
          Thank you for helping me put these
          out again, Ava. I really
          appreciate it.

Ava smiles at her.

                    AVA
          Of course. I'll do whatever I can
          to help find her. Plus, I get to
          spend the day with you.

Chloe smiles as she reaches for another poster from Ava.

                    CHLOE
          Yeah? That's a bonus, huh?

                    AVA
          Abso-fucking-lutely.

Ava holds the posters with one hand, and reaches out with
her other. She grabs Chloe around the back of her neck,
and pulls her close. Ava stares into Chloe's eyes for a
moment.

                    AVA
          God, I love you're eyes. They're
          beautiful. I get lost every time I
          look into them.

Ava kisses her passionately.

The hear a small dog BARK, and pull apart. They see MRS.
THOMPSON, early 60's, with her dog. Mrs. Thompson watches
them intently. Chloe blushes. Ava wipes her mouth.

                    MRS. THOMPSON
          Good morning girls!

                                          (CONTINUED)

CONTINUED:

                         CHLOE
               Sorry about that, Mrs. Thompson.

Mrs. Thompson waves her off.

                         MRS. THOMPSON
               Nothing to be sorry for. Young
               love should be celebrated!

Chloe reaches down and scratches the dog's head.

                         CHLOE
               Good morning, Ace!

Mrs. Thompson nods at the flyer on the pole.

                         MRS. THOMPSON
               I'm guessing she's still missing?

Chloe nods.

                         CHLOE
               Yeah...About a year now.

                         MRS. THOMPSON
               I can't imagine...If there is
               anything you or your dad..

                         CHLOE (INTERRUPTING)
               Ken...his name is Ken.

Ava rubs Chloe's back, in a consoling way.

                         MRS. THOMPSON
               Of course dear. If either of you
               need anything, please let me know.

                         CHLOE
               Thank you.

                         MRS. THOMPSON
               She'll turn up. I'm sure of it.

Mrs. Thompson smiles at them and her dog continue on
their way.

                         AVA
               So..you were a little rude to her.

                         CHLOE
               Was I?

CONTINUED: (2)

                    AVA
          Just a little. You okay?

Chloe shrugs.

                    CHLOE
          I'm okay. Just trying not to think
          too much about it.

Ava puts her hand on Chloe's shoulder.

                    AVA
          It's not healthy to ignore it.

                    CHLOE
          I know. I just wish I had some
          idea of what happened to her.

                    AVA
          Like a clue...or a lead?

                    CHLOE
          Exactly.

                    AVA
          How's your da- Ken doing?

                    CHLOE
          All he does is drink.

                    AVA
          I'm sorry, but try to go easy on
          him. You had me to lean on. He
          doesn't have anyone.

Chloe turns and looks into Ava's eyes.

                    CHLOE
          You know, after I dropped out of
          school, you probably saved me.

Ava smiles, brushes a strand of hair out of Chloe's face.
Chloe leans forward and kisses Ava. They touch foreheads.

                    AVA
          I love you.

Chloe jerks back and glares at Ava, an awkward silence
between them.

                    CHLOE
          Come on. We got posters to put up.

INT. WILLIAMS' HOUSE - LIVING ROOM - DAY

Ken sleeps on the couch. The place is trashed. Food
containers, trash, beer cans, and hard liquor bottles
litter the room. There is a picture of him and Kathy on
the coffee table. Ken's arm hangs off the side of the
couch. Below his hand on the floor is a paper. He dropped
it when he passed out.

The front door opens. Chloe and Ava enter. Chloe looks
around the room in disgust.

                    CHLOE
          Really?

                    AVA
          He didn't clean like he promised.

Chloe sees the paper on the ground. She walks over and
picks it up. She is clearly bothered by what she is
reading. She glares down at Ken.

                    AVA
          Chloe, what is it?

                    CHLOE
          Ken, wake up.

Ken stirs, but doesn't wake.

                    CHLOE
          Ken!

Ken rolls over and faces the back of the couch. Chloe
kicks the front of the couch.

                    CHLOE
          Wake up, now!

Ken shows no signs of life for a moment.

                    KEN
          Do you girls have any aspirin?

                    CHLOE
          What is this?

                    KEN
          What is what?

                    CHLOE
          Turn around and look at me.

                                        (CONTINUED)

CONTINUED:

Ken groans as he turns around and sits up. He squints up
at Chloe, then to Ava.

> KEN
> Get off my case.

Chloe shoves the paper at him. Ken gets serious when he
sees it.

> CHLOE
> Where did this come from?

> KEN
> That's mine. Give it back.

Chloe starts to read from it.

> CHLOE
> "My dearest Ken."

> KEN
> Don't.

> CHLOE
> "I love you more than you can ever
> know. I have to sacrifice this
> amazing life with you for Chloe.
> Take care of her. Protect her.
> She's special."

Ken snatches the paper out of Chloe's hand.

> KEN
> You had no right to read that.

> CHLOE
> It's been a year! You've had that
> this whole time?

Ken grabs a half drunk bottle of beer from the coffee
table, and takes a drink. He avoids looking at her.

> CHLOE
> How could you not tell me?

> KEN
> She left it to me, not you.

Chloe shakes her head, and takes in the room once more.

> CHLOE
> Look at his place. Look at you.
> She wouldn't want this.

CONTINUED: (2)

Ken scoffs, still looking away.

                    KEN
          Don't you tell me what she would
          have wanted. Obviously, neither of
          us had a clue what she wanted.

Ava grabs Chloe's arm.

                    AVA
          Let's just go to your room.

                    KEN
          "I have to sacrifice this amazing
          life with you for Chloe."

                    CHLOE
          What are you saying?

Ken glares at Chloe with red puffy eyes.

                    KEN
          She left because of you.

Chloe looks at him in disbelief.

                    CHLOE
          Maybe she left because of you! You
          didn't appreciate her! You're
          nothing but a pathetic drunk! Of
          course she'd run off with the
          first guy who sent her flowers!

Chloe turns and runs to her room. The door SLAMS. Ken
gets up to follow Chloe.

Ava blocks his path.

                    KEN
          This is none of your business.

                    AVA
          The hell it isn't. I've been the
          one here for her for the last 10
          months, while you've been drowning
          in alcohol and self pity.

Ken calms down a bit. He starts to tear up.

                    KEN
          Look, I just want to tell her that
          I didn't mean it. I'm still drunk,
          and I'm just so angry. All the
          time. God, I miss her.

CONTINUED: (3)

                              AVA
                    I'll tell her. You have no idea
                    how special she is, do you? Get
                    your shit together.

Ava follows Chloe to her room. Ken grabs a beer bottle,
goes to drink it, but it's empty. He throws it against
the wall. It shatters. He leaves.

INT. WILLIAMS' HOUSE - CHLOE'S ROOM - MOMENTS LATER

Ava enters the room and shuts the door. Chloe sits on her
bed, back to the door. A picture of Cathy sits next to
her. Chloe is fighting tears.

                            CHLOE
                    Mom, where are you? I need you.

She picks up the picture.

                            CHLOE
                    Ava told me that she loves me
                    today.

INT. WILLIAMS' HOUSE - HALLWAY OUTSIDE CHLOE'S ROOM -
NIGHT

Ava stands at the door, with her ear to it, listening to
Chloe.

INT. WILLIAMS' HOUSE - CHLOE'S ROOM - NIGHT

                            CHLOE
                    I want to tell her I love her so
                    bad, but I can't. If I tell her,
                    then it's real, and if I love
                    someone, they leave me.

The door opens, and Ava pokes her head in.

                            AVA
                    Hey, You okay?

Chloe quickly hides the picture under a pillow. She wipes
her eyes, and turns to look at Ava.

                            CHLOE
                    He's such an asshole.

Ava comes and sits on the bed next to her.

CONTINUED:

                         AVA
               He told me he didn't mean it. He
               said it was the booze and the
               grief.

                         CHLOE
               Yeah, sure. I can't wait to move
               the fuck out of here. I stayed to
               help him, for mom.

Ava rubs the Chloe's back with her hand.

                         AVA
               Babe, look. He's hurting. You're
               all he has now. You should try to
               be there for him.

Chloe rolls her eyes.

                         AVA
               This isn't about him is it? You
               don't have to hide anything from
               me. What's under the pillow?

                         CHLOE
               Can you just hold me?

Chloe buries her face in Ava's chest as she sobs. Ava
holds her.

INT. BAR - NIGHT

Ken downs a shot of vodka at the bar. Ken scans the bar
from his stool. The only other patron is an OLD MAN,
skinny and pale, in a dark booth. He wears a beat up
fedora. Ken makes eye contact with him. The old man gives
Ken a big sickly grin.

Ken turns around and slides his glass to the BARTENDER.

                         KEN
               Hit me again.

The bartender fills the glass up. Ken reaches for it.

                         KEN
               Who's the fossil?

                         BARTENDER
               I don't know. He started coming in
               about a week ago.

                                              (CONTINUED)

CONTINUED:

                         KEN
               He's fucking creepy.

The bartender chuckles.

                         BARTENDER
               Well, he tips better than you.

The front door opens and TIM, buff, late 40s - early 50s,
enters and sits down next to Ken.

                         TIM
               Sorry I'm late. How deep are you?

Ken downs the glass.

                         KEN
               That was number 3.

He slides the glass back.

                         KEN
               Again.

Tim motions to the bartender.

                         TIM
               Yeah, one for me, too.

Tim looks back at Ken.

                         TIM
               You look like shit. Have you been
               sleeping well?

Ken shrugs.

                         KEN
               Not really. Nightmares started up
               again.

                         TIM
               Oh shit. When?

                         KEN
               About a week after she left. Not 1
               damn nightmare for the 10 years
               while we were together. Now I'm
               back in that fucking war every
               night.

                         TIM
               Sorry, brother.

CONTINUED: (2)

                    KEN
          Only time I don't have them is
          when I'm passed out drunk.

                    TIM
          Shit. How is Chloe?

                    KEN
          I fucked up. Like always.

                    TIM
          Look, you and Chloe are going
          through a hard time...

                    KEN
          Save the bullshit, Tim. I'm here
          to drink, not have a therapy
          session.

Ken looks down at his drink.

                    TIM
          Look, you're like a brother to me,
          Ken. We marines have to stick
          together. Whatever you need, man.
          I'm here for you.

Ken downs his drink.

                    KEN
          Oo-fucking-rah.

He slams his glass on the bar. Ken looks at the
bartender.

                    KEN
          My therapist here will be picking
          up the tab, and the fucking tip.

Ken walks toward the door. Tim watches him.

                    TIM
          Just remember, Chloe's hurting,
          too. Be there for her, Ken.

The old man watches as Ken flips Tim the bird without
looking back as he exits.

                    BARTENDER
          Shame about his wife.

Tim turns and looks at the bartender. He grabs his shot.

CONTINUED: (3)

                         TIM
          Yeah. A damn shame.

                         BARTENDER
          Did she really just up and leave
          them?

Tim downs his drink, as he glares at the bartender.

                         TIM
          What do I owe you?

INT. WILLIAMS' HOUSE - CHLOE'S ROOM - NIGHT

Chloe and Ava lie on Chloe's bed. Chloe's head rests on
Ava's chest. A tv is on with the volume low. The light
bounces off their faces as the watch a show.

                         AVA
          I think I'm going to get a new
          tattoo. On the other shoulder.

                         CHLOE
          Oh yeah?

                         AVA
          Yeah. A dove.

                         CHLOE
          What is your obsession with birds?

                         AVA
          I don't know. They're majestic.
          Beautiful. Powerful.

Chloe laughs.

                         CHLOE
          Powerful?

                         AVA
          Sure. Gravity can't hold them
          down. That's power.

They lay in silence for a few moments.

                         CHLOE
          Why a dove?

                         AVA
          Well, it's you. I'm the raven on
          my right shoulder. The dove on my
          left would represent you.

                                        (CONTINUED)

CONTINUED:

Chloe smiles to herself.

                    CHLOE
          Ava....about earlier... I --

                    AVA
          It's okay. You don't have to say
          it if you're not ready.

                    CHLOE
          Thank you.

Chloe starts to drift off to sleep.

                    AVA
          Your mom's right, you know.

                    CHLOE (GROGGY)
          What?

                    AVA
          The note. She said you're special.

Chloe is asleep. Ava turns off the tv and makes herself
comfortable holding Chloe, and closes her eyes.

INT. WILLIAMS' HOUSE - CHLOE'S ROOM - MORNING

Chloe and Ava sleep in the bed. The door swings open,
revealing Ken standing in the door way.

                    KEN
          Chloe, wake up.

Chloe and Ava stir.

                    CHLOE
          What?

                    KEN
          Someone's here. It's about your
          mom. Hurry up.

Ken leaves. Chloe looks at Ava with hope and fear.

INT. WILLIAMS' HOUSE - KITCHEN - MOMENTS LATER

Chloe and Ava enter the kitchen. At the table sits Ken
and a middle aged man, JACOB, in a suit, with a brief
case on the table. He stands.

                                        (CONTINUED)

CONTINUED:

                    JACOB
          Hello. Please, sit down.

Chloe and Ava sit across from the man. He sits down after
they do.

                    CHLOE
          What's this about?

                    JACOB
          My name is Jacob Montgomery. I'm a
          lawyer, and I've been working for
          your mom for many years.

Chloe looks at Ken. Ken shakes his head and shrugs.

                    CHLOE
          We've never heard of you.

                    JACOB
          I can't speak as to why she never
          mentioned me. I'm here because she
          has now been missing for almost a
          year, and her property must
          legally be passed to an heir.

Jacob opens his briefcase, takes out a folder and hands
it to Ken.

                    JACOB
          Kathy is the owner of a secluded
          cabin in The Ozark Mountains.

Ken pulls out pictures of the cabin from the folder, and
looks them over.

                    CHLOE
          What?

                    KEN
          That's not possible. She would
          have told me about this.

                    JACOB
          I'm assure you, it's very real.
          This cabin now belongs to you.

                    CHLOE
          Where is she?

                    JACOB
          I'm afraid I don't know. She
          hasn't been in contact with me for
          over a year.

CONTINUED: (2)

                    KEN
          What's the name of your firm?

                    JACOB
          Oh! I'm just a small time lawyer,
          I'm the only employee.

Jacob smiles at them, and snaps his briefcase shut.

                    JACOB
          If you'll excuse me, I have other
          business to attend to. Enjoy your
          new property. Let me know if you'd
          like to sell. My number is in the
          folder.

Jacob stands.

                    KEN
          Wait.

Jacob stops and looks at Ken.

                    KEN (CONT'D)
          Can you tell us anything useful?
          How long has she owned this cabin?

                    JACOB
          My understanding is that it's been
          in her family for decades. I'm
          afraid I don't know anything else.
          I hope she turns up soon.

Jacob leaves. The sound of the front door OPENING and
CLOSING is heard.

Chloe looks at Ken.

                    CHLOE
          What the fuck?

                    KEN
          I'm just as shocked and clueless
          as you are, Chloe.

                    CHLOE
          Let me see the pictures.

Ken hands her the folder, and Chloe looks through the
pictures and paper work. Ava looks with her.

                    AVA
          This is good, right?

                                        (CONTINUED)

CONTINUED: (3)

                         KEN
               How could this possibly be good?

Ava looks at Chloe with wide excited eyes.

                         AVA
               Chloe, this is the lead you've
               been asking for, right?

Chloe closes the folder and nods. She looks at Ken.

                         CHLOE
               It's a 12 hour drive. We can get
               there before midnight.

                         KEN
               Absolutely not. We're not going.

                         CHLOE
               Ken! How could we not go? She
               could be there! We could find out
               what happened to her!

Ken leans forward in his chair.

                         KEN
               I said no. She made a choice. She
               walked out that door of her own
               free will.

Chloe bolts to her feet out of her chair.

                         CHLOE
               We have to check this out, Ken.

Ken slams his fist on the table.

                         KEN
               Stop calling me Ken!!

The outburst catches both Chloe and Ava off guard. Ava
slowly stands. Ken composes himself.

                         KEN
               I'm your father.

                         CHLOE
               The fuck you are. Come on, Ava.

Chloe leaves the room, with Ava following behind her. Ken
sits and stares for a moment, and then holds his face in
his hands.

EXT. OUTSIDE WILLIAMS' HOUSE - DAY

Chloe storms out of the house, with Ava following close
behind.

                    AVA
          Chloe! Wait.

Chloe gets out to the street, and starts to pace back and
forth, frustrated. Behind them, the mailman, SEAN, is
coming up the street, getting close to their mailbox.

                    CHLOE
          I don't get it. How could he not
          want to go?

                    AVA
          I know, baby. Just breathe.

Chloe looks back at the house.

                    CHLOE
          Asshole!

                    SEAN
          What'd I do?

They both turn and look at him.

                    CHLOE
          Not you.

                    AVA
          Any fat checks today, Sean?

                    SEAN
          I'm afraid not. They all look like
          junk mail today.

Sean hands a small stack of envelopes to Chloe. She takes
them with a weak smile.

                    SEAN
          Hey Chloe. I just wanted you to
          know that I took one of your
          flyers, about your mom. I made
          hundreds of copies, and I give
          them out with the mail.

Chloe's eyes light up.

                    CHLOE
          Oh my goodness! That is so sweet!

(CONTINUED)

CONTINUED:

Chloe hugs Sean.

                    SEAN
          Every house on my route has at
          least one flyer.

                    CHLOE
          Thank you so much.

Sean nods.

                    SEAN
          It's the least I could do. I hope
          they find her. You two have a good
          day.

Sean makes his way to the next mailbox.

                    AVA
          See. Everyone's looking for her.
          We'll find her.

INT. WILLIAMS' HOUSE - LIVING ROOM - DAY

Ken and Tim are sitting on the couch having a beer
together.

                    TIM
          A random cabin? In the middle of
          nowhere?

                    KEN
          Yep. I had no idea.

                    TIM
          I understand Chloe wanting to go.
          Why don't you?

Ken takes a slow drink of beer.

                    KEN
          She didn't tell me about this
          cabin, Tim. What else didn't she
          tell me about. If I go looking for
          her, I'm afraid I won't like what
          I find.

                    TIM
          What are you afraid of finding?

                    KEN
          Look, the way I see it, this ends
          a couple of ways.
                    (MORE)

CONTINUED:

                    KEN (CONT'D)
          Either she's dead, or she's not
          the person I thought she was.

Ken sighs and turns to examine his beer bottle.

                    KEN
          Or worse. Chloe's right, and she
          left because of me.

Ken looks up at Tim, fighting tears.

                    KEN
          I don't think I could handle any
          of those.

INT. WILLIAM'S HOUSE - CHLOE'S ROOM - NIGHT

Chloe and Ava are sitting on the bed. Chloe is looking
through the pictures of the cabin, and Ava is reading a
book.

                    CHLOE
          The whole situation aside, this
          cabin looks awesome.

Ava looks up from her book.

                    AVA
          Yeah, It does.

                    CHLOE
          I can't stop thinking that she
          might be there.

Ava shuts the book, and scoots closer to Chloe.

                    AVA
          Chloe, look at me. Let me see
          those beautiful eyes of yours.

Chloe turns and makes eye contact. They both smile.

                    AVA
          We don't need Ken. We are grown
          ass women. If you want to go, I'm
          with you.

                    CHLOE
          Oh my god! Really?!

                    AVA
          Of course, bitch. I gotchu.

CONTINUED:

                    CHLOE
          Can we go now?

                    AVA
          I thought you'd never ask.

Chloe excitedly kisses Ava, passionately.

                    AVA
          Well, maybe not RIGHT NOW.

Ava moves under the covers. Chloe GASPS.

                    CHLOE
     Oh....

INT. WILLIAM'S HOUSE - CHLOE'S ROOM - DAY

The room is empty. Pictures of the cabin are strewn
across the bed. There is a KNOCK on the door.

                    KEN (O.S.)
          Chloe! You in there? We should
          talk about things.

Ken opens the door and sees the empty room. He sees the
pictures on the bed.

                    KEN
     Sonofabitch.

EXT. OUTSIDE WILLIAMS' HOUSE - DAY

Ken is walking to his car on his phone, carrying a small
travel bag.

                    KEN
          Tim! Listen, Chloe went to the
          cabin.

                    TIM (O.S.)
          By herself?

                    KEN
          I'm sure Ava is with her, but
          whatever she finds out there, I
          can't let her face it alone. I'm
          going after them.

                    TIM (O.S.)
          How far behind them are you?

                                             (CONTINUED)

CONTINUED:

                    KEN
          I don't know. They aren't
          answering their phones.

                    TIM (O.S.)
          Okay. Be careful. Let me know if I
          can help in anyway.

                    KEN
          Thanks.

Ken hangs up and gets into his car

INT. CABIN - LIVING ROOM - DAY

Dust particles float in the light from the windows. It's
quiet, and ominous. The room is filled with primitive
tools: Candles, lanterns. Old books stand at attention on
an old book shelf. A large rug covers the floor.

The door bursts open, shattering the peace. Chloe and Ava
enter, each carrying a few bags. They set the bags down.

Ava slowly walks around the room, taking in everything.
Chloe plays with a lantern on the table in the middle of
the room.

                    CHLOE
          This place is cool.

                    AVA
          Would have been a fun place for
          family trips. I wonder why your
          mom kept it a secret.

                    CHLOE
          Lets search the rest of the place.

INT. CABIN - BEDROOM - DAY

Ava enters the room, and looks around the room. The room
is empty except for the bed and a dresser. She opens the
first drawer. It's empty, she closes it. She opens the
second drawer. There is an old picture frame sitting face
down. She picks it up, and turns it over. It is of Kathy
and Ruth when they were younger.

                    AVA
          Chloe!

Chloe rushes into the room.

CONTINUED:

                    CHLOE
          What?

Ava shows Chloe the picture.

                    AVA
          Is that your mom?

                    CHLOE
          I think so...when she was younger.

Chloe turns and looks the room over again.

                    CHLOE
          So, she did live here. Who is the
          other girl? I saw another room.
          I'm going to go check it out.

Ava nods, as she turns to further inspect the room.

INT. CABIN - 2ND BEDROOM - DAY

Chloe enters the room. It is mostly empty. There is a
small desk with papers and books on it. There is a bed,
with old red stains on the sheets. Chloe's eyes widen
when she sees it.

                    CHLOE
          Ava!

Ava rushes in. Chloe points to the bed.

                    CHLOE
          Does that look like blood to you?

Ava walks closer to the bed to look at it closer.

                    AVA
          Could be. Its old. The sheets have
          been stained for a while.

The desk of papers catches Chloe's attention. She walks
over, and starts looking at things on the desk. They are
documents and books about the demon Malphas. The Sigil of
Malphas is all over these books and documents.

                    CHLOE
          What the fuck?

Ava comes up beside her.

                    AVA
          Holy shit.

CONTINUED:

Chloe looks at Ava.

                    CHLOE
          What the hell was my mom into?

INT. CABIN - KITCHEN - DAY

Chloe and Ava have the books and papers spread out over
the table, and they are reading through them.

                    CHLOE
          This says that Malphas is one of
          the most powerful demons. 2nd in
          command under Satan.

Chloe flips the page and sees a drawing of Malphas. He is
depicted as a bird humanoid. Chloe snorts.

                    CHLOE
          He's a fucking bird.

                    AVA
          Hey! Don't knock birds. They're
          deceptively powerful.

                    CHLOE
          I'm just saying. He's not very
          intimidating, for a demon.

Something catches Ava's attention on the paper she's
scanning.

                    AVA
          What kind of flowers did you say
          your mom got when she left?

                    CHLOE
          Marigolds.

Ava looks up at Chloe and raises the paper in her hand.

                    AVA
          Marigolds are his plant.

                    CHLOE
          Oh my god. My mom is mixed up in
          all this. What is happening?

Ava reaches across the table and takes Chloe's hand.

                                        (CONTINUED)

CONTINUED:

                         AVA
               I don't know, but we're going to
               find out, and I'm not about to
               leave your side.

INT. CABIN - BEDROOM - NIGHT

Chloe and Ava are in bed. Ava is sleeping, Chloe is
reading through the book about Malphas.

                         CHLOE
               Holy shit.

Ava stirs. She looks up at Chloe, and sighs, and flops
her head back on the pillow.

                         AVA
               Go to sleep.

                         CHLOE
               Ava, I think we might need to go.

Ava sleepily raises her head.

                         AVA
               What?

Chloe turns the page, getting more frightened.

                         CHLOE
               This talks about a ritual. Some
               kind of summoning ceremony for
               Malphas, where he take control of
               a vessel.

                         AVA
               So?

Chloe looks at Ava, eyes wide.

                         CHLOE
               The vessel has to have
               heterochromia.

                         AVA
               Oh shit.

                         CHLOE
               It says it makes it easier for the
               demon, because the windows to the
               soul are open.

CONTINUED:

                        AVA
Eyes are the windows to the soul.

                        CHLOE
Exactly.

                        AVA
Okay. We'll leave first thing in
the morning.

                        CHLOE
It says that Malphas is strongest
on October 5th.

                        AVA
Tomorrow. They'll want to do it
when he is at his strongest.

                        CHLOE
That's what I'm thinking. If any
of these people are still around,
we're in serious danger. We should
leave now.

Ava gets up out of bed.

                        AVA
Okay.

EXT. OUTSIDE CABIN - NIGHT

Chloe and Ava exit the cabin door, and start to head to
their car. Headlights spotlight them as another vehicle
drives up the driveway. The drivers side door opens, and
Ken steps out.

                        CHLOE
Ken! What are you doing here?

                        KEN
Coming after your disobedient ass.
Where are you going?

                        CHLOE
We have to leave.

                        KEN
Why? What did you find?

                        CHLOE
We just have to go. I'll tell you
all about it later.

CONTINUED:

                    KEN
          I just drove 12 hours. We are
          going inside, and you're going to
          tell me what's going on.

Chloe looks at Ava.

                    AVA
          He has a right to know. We should
          probably tell him. A few more
          minutes won't hurt.

INT. CABIN - KITCHEN - NIGHT

Ken, Chloe, and Ava sit at the kitchen table, as Ken
leafs through the papers and book.

                    KEN
          You think your mom is some sort of
          devil worshiper?

                    CHLOE
          I don't know. This might not even
          be hers, but this cabin is, and we
          found it here.

                    KEN
          Why were you so anxious to leave?

                    CHLOE
          Are you not listening? Whoever
          these people are, then are looking
          for someone with Heterochromia!

Chloe motions to her eyes.

                    CHLOE
          Hello!

                    KEN
          You know demons aren't real.

                    CHLOE
          Maybe not, but crazy ass people
          who worship them are! Can we go?!

Ken nods.

                    KEN
          Okay. We'll get a hotel room on
          the way home.

CONTINUED:

The stand up. POUNDING on the front door is heard. Ava and Chloe scream.

                    KEN
          What the fuck?

INT. CABIN - LIVING ROOM - NIGHT

The room is dark. Ken, Chloe, and Ava slowly walk into the living room, with their focus on the front door. POUNDING is heard again.

                    CHLOE
          Ken?

                    KEN
          Shhh. It's okay. I won't let
          anything happen to you.

                    AVA
          I'm scared.

                    KEN
          Whoever you are, get the fuck out
          of here!

The pounding stops. Moments of silence slice the air.

                    JULIAN (O.S.)
          We want the girl.

Ken turns and looks at Chloe, then Ava, and back to the door.

                    KEN
          Why?

                    JULIAN (O.S.)
          The window to her soul is open.
          She is his vessel.

Chloe starts to tear up.

                    CHLOE
          Shit. It's them. They're going to
          kill me.

                    KEN
          It's going to be okay.

                    JULIAN (O.S.)
          The girl, and you will live.

CONTINUED:

                    KEN
          How about you get the fuck out of
          here, and you will live!

Ken slowly walks to the a front window. Behind Chloe and
Ava, TWO FIGURES in black hoods slowly emerge from the
darkness.

Ken looks out the window. There are 2 MEN in black cloaks
with skull masks.

                    KEN
          Shit.

The two figures behind the girls grab each of them from
behind. They both SCREAM. Each hooded figure holds a
knife to each girl's throat.

Ken spins around.

                    KEN
          Let them go!

The front door opens, Julian walks into the room followed
by the other man in the skull mask. Julian takes his mask
off to reveal the old man that was in the bar. He smiles
his creepy smile.

                    JULIAN
          We meet again, my friend.

It takes Ken a minute to recognize him.

                    KEN
          What the fuck? You've been
          following me?

                    JULIAN
          "Sacrifice and offering you did
          not desire, but a body you
          prepared for me."

                    KEN
          What?

                    JULIAN
          Hebrews. 10:5. Tell me, Ken.

Julian walks toward Ken.

                    KEN
          Back the fuck up!

CONTINUED: (2)

                    JULIAN
          What would you sacrifice for a
          better world?

                    KEN
          Let the girls go.

                    JULIAN
          Unfortunately, I can't do that.
          Frank.

The other man takes his mask off. Frank smiles at Ken.

                    JULIAN
          Ken, this is my associate, Frank.

Frank pulls out a crowbar from inside his cloak.

                    JULIAN
          Frank is the welcoming party in
          these parts.

                    KEN
          What the fuck do you want?

                    JULIAN
          I've already told you. We're
          taking the girls. Both of them.

Ava cries.

                    CHLOE
          What about Ken?

Julian walks over to Chloe.

                    KEN
          Well, Frank here is going to give
          Ken a nice warm welcome.

Frank swings the crowbar at Ken. Ken blocks it with his
arm. Ken GRUNTS and stumbles but doesn't fall down.

                    CHLOE
          Ken! No!

Ken lunges at Frank, and grabs him by the throat.

                    JULIAN
          Stop!

Ken looks at Julian while holding Frank by his throat.

CONTINUED: (3)

> JULIAN
> Are you sure you're willing to
> sacrifice you Chloe?

Ken looks at Chloe. The figure holding her slides his blade slightly across her neck, drawing a sliver of blood. Chloe CRIES out.

> KEN
> I'm going to kill every one of you
> fucking bastards.

Ken lets go of Frank's throat.

Frank takes another swing, hitting Ken in the jaw. Ken stumbles back.

> CHLOE
> No! Ken! Stop it!

Frank takes his crowbar and slams Ken on the top of the head with it. Ken crumples to the ground.

> CHLOE
> DAD!!

Ken surges to his feet at the sound of the word. He takes a disoriented swing at Frank. Frank dodges it, and swings the crowbar into Ken's ribs. Ken cries out, and falls to the ground.

Frank kicks Ken in the ribs and stomach over and over, until Ken stops moving and making noise.

Chloe and Ava cry.

> CHLOE
> Dad! No! Get up!

Julian smiles at Chloe.

> JULIAN
> We've been waiting a long time for
> you, my dear. Frank, dispose of
> our unwanted guest.

> FRANK
> My pleasure. Cell phones.

The 2 figures take Chloe and Ava's phones and give them to Frank.

> JULIAN
> Let's get our girls home.

CONTINUED: (4)

Julian leads the 2 hooded figures, and the girls out of
the cabin.

Frank stands over Ken.

EXT. COMPOUND - NIGHT

Julian leads both hooded figures, each still holding Ava
and Chloe. The emerge from a path in the woods to a small
compound of old wood buildings. One is a church.

                          AVA
             Where are we?

Julian turns around and looks at her. He smiles.

                          JULIAN
             Home.

Julian turns the hooded figure holding Ava.

                          JULIAN
             Sean, go prepare the sanctuary.

Sean, pulls his hood down, he turns and smiles at Chloe.
She GASPS in horror as she recognizes him.

                          AVA
             Oh my god!

                          SEAN
             Sorry, girls. No fat checks today,
             either.

Sean heads toward the church.

                          CHLOE
             What?

Julian laughs.

                          JULIAN
             My dear child. You have no idea
             whats happening, do you?

                          CHLOE
             Is my mom here? What have you done
             with her?!

                                              (CONTINUED)

CONTINUED:

                    JULIAN
          Yes. Your mother is here. You'll
          see her soon, and all your
          questions will be answered, I
          promise, my child.

Chloe start to sob hysterically.

                    AVA
          Chloe, look at me.

Chloe looks at Ava with tears streaking her cheeks.

                    AVA
          Baby, breathe. We're going to be
          okay. I'm here. Just breathe.

                    JULIAN
          Touching. Your new home together
          awaits.

EXT. BEHIND CABIN - NIGHT

Frank digs in a shallow grave with a shovel. Ken's
motionless body lies next to the hole. Frank climbs out
of the hole, and thrusts the shovel into the ground.

He rolls Ken into the hole. He grabs the shovel, and
shovels dirt onto Ken.

INT. WILLIAM'S HOUSE KEN'S BEDROOM - NIGHT

Ken sleeps in bed, as Kathy packs a suitcase. Ken stirs,
he lifts his head and looks at her sleepily.

                    KEN
          Kathy? Honey, what are you doing?

Kathy looks at him as she tosses some clothes into the
suitcase.

                    KATHY
          I'm leaving you.

Ken puzzles for a moment.

                    KEN
          But, you already left.

                                              (CONTINUED)

CONTINUED:

                    KATHY
          After everything I did for you.
          After all I put up with and
          sacrificed! You can't wake your
          lazy ass up!

GUNFIRE erupts from the bathroom. Looks toward the
bathroom. 3 DEAD SOLDIERS walk out of a mist towards him
out of the bathroom.

                    KEN
          What the fuck?

They reach out toward him.

                    KATHY
          You left them, Ken! You left them
          to die, you piece of shit!

The zombies shamble closer.

                    ZOMBIE #1
          Keeeennnn........

                    KEN
          I'm so fucking sorry! Stop! I'm
          sorry.

                    KATHY
          You can't leave Chloe to die, too!
          Wake up, you sonofabitch! Wake the
          fuck up!

EXT. BEHIND CABIN - NIGHT

The still night settles over Ken's freshly dug grave.
Near the grave is a pile of smashed cell phones. Ken's
hand bursts out of the dirt, reaching up into the night.
He grabs the ground, and pulls himself into a seated
position, and gasps for air.

EXT. OUTSIDE CABIN - NIGHT

Frank is sitting in the drivers seat of his car on his
cell phone. His window is down.

                    FRANK
          Yeah Julian, It's done. He's in
          the ground. Okay. I'll keep an eye
          on things from the station.
                    (MORE)

CONTINUED:

                    FRANK (CONT'D)
          Protect you, and make sure the
          ceremony isn't disturbed. Hail
          Malphas!

Frank hangs up. He adjusts the rearview mirror and
momentarily sees Ken illuminated by the break lights.
Frank spins his head around to look, but no one is there.

                    FRANK
          What the fuck?

Frank CRIES OUT as Ken grabs him through the drivers side
window. Ken drags him through the window and drops him on
the ground.

                    KEN
          You fucked up, asshole!

Ken stomps on Frank's face.

INT. CHURCH - NIGHT

Chloe and Ava are each chained to the wall of the church.
Ava is chained up closer to the door than Chloe. The
church is a demonic shrine to Malphas. There is a table
with a large metal bowl, and animal skulls on it.
Marigold flowers decorate the sanctuary. No one else is
in the room.

                    AVA
          Can you get free?

Chloe tries to slip her wrists through the chains, then
pulls on them.

                    CHLOE
          I don't think so.

The door bursts open. Mrs. Thompson walks in holding a
tray with two bowls of food. She sees Chloe and smiles.

                    CHLOE
          What? Mrs. Thompson?

                    MRS. THOMPSON
          I've got some food for you girls.

Mrs. Thompson sets a bowl down in front of Ava. Ava
glares at her. Mrs. Thompson smiles back.

                    MRS. THOMPSON
          Gorgeous little thing.

CONTINUED:

She smiles at Chloe.

                    MRS. THOMPSON
          You know, Chloe, I don't blame
          you. If I was a few decades
          younger, I might take a go at her.

Mrs. Thompson sets the second bowl down in front of
Chloe, and watches them for a moment.

                    MRS. THOMPSON
          Well, go on. You must be hungry.

Both Ava and Chloe continue to sit there and look at her.

                    MRS. THOMPSON
          Oh for pete's sake. It's safe.

Mrs. Thompson takes a spoon full of soup from each bowl
to prove it's safe. Chloe and Ava reluctantly eat.

                    AVA
          How long have you all been
          watching us?

                    MRS. THOMPSON
          Oh, It's not you that we've been
          watching.

Mrs. Thompson looks at Chloe.

                    MRS. THOMPSON
          It's her.

                    CHLOE
          What do you want?

Mrs. Thompson turns and starts to gather the tray.

                    MRS. THOMPSON
          All in good time, dear. Elder
          Julian will explain everything.

Mrs. Thompson smiles a friendly old lady smile.

                    MRS. THOMPSON
          Nice to see you again, dears.

INT. CABIN - LIVING ROOM - NIGHT

Frank is unconscious and tied up to a chair in the middle
of the living room.

                                        (CONTINUED)

CONTINUED:

Frank has a footprint shaped bruise across his face. Ken is standing in front of him, looking through Frank's wallet. Frank's ID shows that he's the local sheriff.

                    KEN
          Wake up, you piece of shit!

Ken smacks Frank across the face. Frank wakes up. He sees Ken, and struggles against the ropes.

                    KEN
          You're not getting out. Basically,
          you're fucked.

                    FRANK
          Do you know who I am?!

                    KEN
          You're the dumbass that buried me
          alive. Now, you can either tell me
          where my daughter is and die
          quickly, or I make you tell me. I
          promise you, you won't enjoy it.

                    FRANK
          I'm not telling you shit!

Ken reaches behind his back, and pulls out a rusty pair of pliers.

                    KEN
          I found this in one of the
          drawers. Last chance.

Frank spits in Ken's face. Ken smiles and wipes it off.

                    KEN
          I was hoping you'd say that.

Ken grabs hold of Frank's pinky fingernail with the pliers, and rips it off. Frank SCREAMS.

                    KEN
          You've got 9 more chances. Where's
          my daughter.

INT. CHURCH - NIGHT

Chloe and Ava are sitting as close together as they can. There is about a foot between them.

                    CHLOE
          Do you think Ken's dead?

CONTINUED:

                    AVA
          It didn't look good, Chloe.

Chloe starts to tear up.

                    CHLOE
          I was so hateful to him. I can't
          imagine the horrors he went
          through in the war, and I treated
          him like shit.

                    AVA
          He loved you.

Chloe nods.

                    CHLOE
          Maybe. But I'm not sure he ever
          knew that I loved him.

Chloe looks into Ava's eyes.

                    CHLOE
          Ava, whatever happens, I need to
          say....

Ava shakes her head.

                    AVA
          You don't have to say it....

                    CHLOE
          Thank you for being there for me
          this past year.

                    AVA
          I'm not going anywhere.

Ava smiles at her. The door opens, and Julian enters,
grinning.

                    JULIAN
          Pardon me, hate to interrupt.

                    AVA
          Leave us the fuck alone, you
          creep!

                    CHLOE
          What do you want?

                    JULIAN
          Prepare yourself, Chloe. Tonight
          at midnight, we begin.

                                        (CONTINUED)

CONTINUED: (2)

                    CHLOE
          Midnight? October 5th.

Julian smiles.

                    JULIAN
          That's right! He is most powerful
          on October 5th. That's why we had
          to wait and watch you for so long.

                    CHLOE
          What are you going to do to me?

Julian's smile somehow gets wider and more grotesque.

                    JULIAN
          The ritual has 3 phases. The first
          phase is simple enough. A standard
          blood sacrifice to summon Malphas.
          The 2nd phase is a little more
          complicated. The vessel must
          willingly invite Malphas to
          inhabit them.

Chloe's head snaps up with defiance in her eyes.

                    CHLOE
          I will never do that, no matter
          how bad you torture me. Never!

Julian smiles, and looks at Ava.

                    JULIAN
          Who said anything about torturing
          you?

Chloe looks at Ava.

                    CHLOE
          No.....

Ava slumps back in despair.

                    AVA
          And that's why I'm still alive.

                    JULIAN
          Smart girl.

                    CHLOE
          What's the third phase?

CONTINUED: (3)

                    JULIAN
          Malphas' most devoted follower
          must sacrifice themselves for Him.
          This act of ultimate love
          completes and sanctifies the
          ritual.

                    AVA
          Why are you doing this?

                    JULIAN
          The glory of Malphas, of course!

                    CHLOE
          He's a fucking demon!

                    JULIAN
          Have you ever considered where
          that label came from? Malphas is a
          builder. He will build a beautiful
          utopia on earth. Does that sound
          like something a 'demon' would do?

                    CHLOE
          You're crazy.

Julian smiles.

                    JULIAN
          We'll see. It's almost midnight. I
          must prepare our special guest!

INT. CABIN - LIVING ROOM - NIGHT

Frank SCREAMS as Ken rips off his last fingernail on his
right hand. His thumbnail. Ken drops the nail to the
floor.

                    FRANK
          Please stop! I don't know
          anything.

                    KEN
          Bullshit. I won't stop when I
          finish your fingernails. You also
          have 10 toenails.

Ken grabs the pinky fingernail on Frank's left hand, and
rips it off. Frank SCREAMS.

                    KEN
          We're just getting started.

                                        (CONTINUED)

CONTINUED:

                    FRANK
          We...have a compound.

                    KEN
          Good boy. Where?

                    FRANK
          It's hidden deep in the woods.
          About 2 miles east of here.

                    KEN
          And this is about some bullshit
          about my daughter and her eyes?

Frank laughs.

                    FRANK
          It's not bullshit, and she's not
          your daughter.

Ken punches him in the face. Frank is bleeding from the
nose and mouth.

                    KEN
          How many are at the compound?

                    FRANK
          You'll never get to her. There's
          too many.

Ken grabs Frank's left ring fingernail with the pliers.

                    FRANK
          Okay! Stop!

The pliers release the fingernail.

                    FRANK
          About a dozen or so.

                    KEN
          Any guns?

                    FRANK
          No.

Ken sets the pliers down.

                    KEN
          You're a real son of a bitch, you
          know that? You're a fucking cop,
          for chrissakes!

CONTINUED: (2)

                    FRANK
          I believe in Malphas! He will
          build a new wonderful world!

Ken stands up, and walks around behind Frank.

                    FRANK
          What are you doing?

                    KEN
          Tell your piece of shit god, I'll
          be sending more.

Ken snakes his arms around Frank's neck and head.

                    FRANK
          No! No!

With a CRACK, Ken breaks Frank's neck.

INT. CABIN - KITCHEN - NIGHT

Ken has a machete and a few hunting knives on the table.
The papers and books about Malphas still liter the table
as well.

Ken dials a number on Frank's cell phone.

                    TIM (O.S.)
          Hello?

                    KEN
          Thank God! It's Ken.

                    TIM (O.S.)
          What's wrong?

                    KEN
          I found Chloe and Ava at the
          cabin, then this fucking demon
          cult attacked us. They took Chloe!

                    TIM (O.S.)
          What?

Ken takes a deep breath to calm himself.

                    KEN
          They beat me unconscious. Tim,
          they fucking buried me! The took
          Chloe and Ava.

CONTINUED:

                    TIM
          Jesus, Ken, you've got to go to
          the police!

                    KEN
          No! One of these fuckers was the
          local sheriff. The leader is that
          old creepy fucker from the bar. I
          can't trust anyone but you.

                    TIM (O.S.)
          Shit. Where are you? I'm on my
          way.

                    KEN
          I'll send the cabin's address.
          They're compound is 2 miles east
          through the woods.

                    TIM (O.S.)
          Ken, how long is the drive?

Ken sighs.

                    KEN
          About 12 hours.

                    TIM (O.S.)
          Ken...I won't be there until
          tomorrow morning at the earliest.

                    KEN
          I know.

                    TIM (O.S.)
          Ken, I need you to wait for me.

Ken considers this a beat.

                    KEN
          She called me "Dad", Tim. For the
          first time. They were beating the
          life out of me in front of her,
          and she called me "Dad."

                    TIM (O.S.)
          Fuck. It sounds like a suicide
          mission, brother.

                    KEN
          She's my daughter. I would stroll
          into the depths of Hell and lay
          down my soul at Satan's feet to
          protect her.

CONTINUED: (2)

           TIM (O.S.)
Do you at least have weapons?

Ken looks down at the weapons on the table.

           KEN
I found a few things around the
cabin. They smashed our phones so
I'm using the cops phone. I don't
know if they have the capability
to track it, but I'm smashing it
as soon as we're done.

           TIM (O.S.)
Understood. I'll be there as quick
as I can. Be careful.

           KEN
Ooooo-fucking-rah.

INT. CHURCH - NIGHT

The door opens, Chloe and Ava leap to their feet. Julian
enters followed by Sean and a hooded CULTIST, both in
cult hoods and robes. They carry candles.

           JULIAN
It's midnight. The time has
finally come to begin!

Behind him, Sean and they cultist are preparing an altar.
They set down the candles on a table next to the large
bowl on the table. Different skulls decorate the table.

           CHLOE
Just let us go!

Julian smiles.

           JULIAN
But you haven't found what you
came for.

           CHLOE
What?

           JULIAN
Jacob!

Jacob, the lawyer from earlier enters, leading a woman
with a sack over her head by a rope that also has her
hands tied. The woman is gagged.

           (CONTINUED)

CONTINUED:

                         AVA
                  (whispers)
            Oh my god.

                         CHLOE
            You?

                         JACOB
            We had to get you out here, now
            didn't we?

                         CHLOE
            It was a lie?

                         JACOB
            No. The cabin does belong to your
            mother and her family.

Julian takes the rope from Jacob. He motions to Ava.

                         JULIAN
            Get her out of here. This is a
            family affair.

Jacob unlocks Ava's chain, and grabs her.

                         JACOB
            Come on.

Ava struggles against him.

                         AVA
            Get your hands off me!

                         CHLOE
            Don't hurt her!
                  (to Ava)
            It's okay.

Ava stops, and follows Jacob out the door. Sean and the
cultist finish preparing the altar.

                         JULIAN
            Leave us!

The Sean and the cultist leave, leaving only Jacob,
Chloe, and the woman with the sack over her head in the
room. Julian smiles at Chloe.

                         CHLOE
            Who's under there?

The woman tries again to talk, but it's muffled. She
struggles against her bindings.

                                        (CONTINUED)

CONTINUED: (2)

                    JULIAN
          Oh, I think you can guess.

Julian slowly grabs the top of the sack, and takes the
sack off, revealing Chloe's mother, Kathy, gagged, her
face bruised and tear streaked. She looks malnourished
and dehydrated.

                    CHLOE
          Mom!

She tries to say something back, but the gag keeps her
from speaking.

                    JULIAN
          Oh! My apologies.

Julian removes the gag.

                    KATHY
          Chloe! Baby! I'm so sorry!

                    CHLOE
          Mom, what is happening?

                    KATHY
          They weren't supposed to know
          about you! I tried to protect you!

                    JULIAN
          But we found out, didn't we? And
          it's all thanks to you.

INT. CABIN - BEDROOM - DAY - FLASHBACK - ONE YEAR AGO

Kathy lays in bed, eyes open, staring at the ceiling,
almost comatose. The door swings open, and her sister,
Ruth enters.

                    RUTH
          Kathy?

Kathy sits up and looks at Ruth, considerably older, as
if she's a stranger.

                    KATHY
          Ruth?

                    RUTH
          Oh, Kathy!

Ruth hurries to the bed, and hugs Kathy tightly. Kathy
slowly hugs her back. They part after a moment.

                                        (CONTINUED)

CONTINUED:

                    RUTH
          There wasn't a day you weren't in
          my thoughts. I wish I had gone
          with you.

                    KATHY
          Why didn't you?

Ruth shrugs.

                    RUTH
          I don't know. Scared, I s'pose.
          but don't worry! I didn't tell
          them anything.

                    KATHY
          How did they find me?

They don't notice a shadow darken the doorway.

                    RUTH
          I don't know exactly. Julian never
          stopped looking for you. Jacob was
          the one who finally found you.

                    KATHY
          You didn't tell them anything?

Ruth shakes her head.

                    RUTH
          No. I swear.

                    KATHY
          They don't know about -

Ruth quickly puts her finger to her lips, with fear in
her eyes.

                    RUTH
          Shhhhh!!!!

The shadow in the doorway morphs into Julian as he walks
into the light of the room.

                    JULIAN
          Don't know about what?

Ruth and Kathy look at each other with panic. Julian
pulls out a decorative knife. He walks to Kathy.

                    JULIAN
          What have you been hiding from us
          all these years?

CONTINUED: (2)

Julian runs the blade down the side of Kathy's face.

                    KATHY
          Nothing! It's nothing.

                    JULIAN
          Oh! Nothing? That's a relief.

Julian turns to Ruth.

                    JULIAN
          Is that true, Ruth? It is nothing?

Ruth hesitates.

                    KATHY
          Ruth, please...

Julian explodes with anger, and turns back to Kathy.

                    JULIAN
          PLEASE?! RUTH PLEASE?! That
          desperation doesn't sound like
          'nothing' to me!

Kathy cowers.

                    KATHY
          I swear, it's nothing.

Julian turns back to Ruth.

                    JULIAN
          I'm going to slowly carve little
          Ruth up, until she tells me what
          the big secret is.

                    RUTH
          No!

We hold on Kathy's face as she watches. Ruth SCREAMS.

                    KATHY
          Stop!

We hear the blade SLICING, and Ruth SCREAMING. Kathy is
crying.

                    RUTH (O.S.)
          The child lived! She had the eyes!

Kathy's eyes close.

(CONTINUED)

CONTINUED: (3)

                    KATHY
          No....

INT. CHURCH - NIGHT

Julian is still holding Kathy.

                    KATHY
          You killed my sister.

                    JULIAN
          No...you did. We are all dealing
          with the consequences of your
          choices.

                    KATHY
          Fuck you!

Julian pulls back on Kathy's hair in anger.

                    JULIAN
          What happened to you?! You used to
          believe! You were devout!

                    KATHY
          I looked into her eyes, and I knew
          I had to save her. Even if it
          meant sacrificing myself.

Julian pulls tighter. Kathy SCREAMS.

                    CHLOE
          Stop! Leave her alone!

                    JULIAN
          What about me? Didn't I deserve a
          say in it?

Julian looks up at Chloe, he smiles.

                    JULIAN
          I did say this was a family
          affair, remember?

Horror creeps across Chloe's face.

                    CHLOE
          No...

                    KATHY
          You bastard.

                                        (CONTINUED)

CONTINUED:

                    JULIAN
          I can't express how much of an
          honor it is that the vessel of
          Malphas is my daughter!

                    CHLOE
          NOO!!!

Kathy is sobbing.

                    KATHY
          Chloe, baby, I'm so sorry.

                    JULIAN
          Enough! It's time to begin!

Julian drags Kathy to the altar. She SCREAMS, and
struggles. She elbows Julian in the gut, and runs to the
door, she opens and runs out as Julian recovers.

Sean and Jacob throw her back through the door. Jacob
grabs her, as Sean guards the door.

Jacob drags her back to the altar with Julian. Julian
pulls out his decorative knife. Jacob holds Kathy's head
over the bowl.

                    JULIAN
          Let phase one of the ritual begin!
          The summoning sacrifice!

Chloe pulls on her chains, trying to break free.

                    CHLOE
          NO!!! Mom!

                    JULIAN
          Lord Malphas! Please accept this
          offering and grace us with your
          magnificent spirit. We spill this
          blood with awe and honor of your
          mighty power!

Julian slits Kathy's throat, and her blood starts to pour
into the bowl. Kathy's screams turn into gurgles.

                    CHLOE
          Mom!!!

                    JULIAN
          We summon you, Malphas!

                    MAILMAN AND JACOB
          We summon you, Malphas!

                                        (CONTINUED)

CONTINUED: (2)

Kathy's body finally goes limp, as her blood has been
drained. Julian lets her body fall to the floor.

A gust of wind fills the room. The candles blow out, and
the door SLAMS shut. A monstrous transparent form can be
seen in the darkness of a corner. Chloe GASPS.

                    JULIAN
          He's here!

EXT. COMPOUND - WOODS - NIGHT

Ken steps out of the shadows of the woods on the
outskirts of the compound. He watches with a hunting
knife in hand. The machete hands from a belt on his side.

Ken watches as as several people in hoods walk back and
forth between the buildings. Ken starts toward the
compound.

INT. COMPOUND CELL ROOM - NIGHT

Chloe, on her knees, staring trance-like at the body of
her mother. She is in shock. Julian opens the front door.

                    JULIAN
          Bring in the girlfriend.

Sean brings in Ava. Julian grabs her, and chains her to
the wall again. Ava hurries to get as close to Chloe as
she can. She reaches out to her.

                    AVA
          Chloe! I'm here!

Chloe continues to stare at her mom's body. Ava sees
Kathy's body.

                    AVA
          Oh my God! Chloe, don't look at
          her! Look at me!

Chloe slowly turns and looks at Ava.

                    CHLOE
          Ava?

                    AVA
          Yes! Yes, It's me, honey. I'm
          here!

CONTINUED:

                    CHLOE
          He killed my mom!

                     AVA
          I know, baby. I know, but I'm here
          now.

                   JULIAN
          How sweet, but we have to move on
          to phase two, Chloe. You have to
          invite Malphas into your body.

Chloe seems to draw strength from Ava. She stands and
faces Julian.

                   CHLOE
          That's never going to happen.

Julian smiles at her. Sinister and hideous.

                   JULIAN
          Oh, I'm afraid that you'll find
          that we can be quite persuasive.

Julian nods at Jacob. Jacob punches Ava in the face,
knocking her down.

                   CHLOE
          Stop! Leave her alone!

Julian shows off his bloody dagger.

                   JULIAN
          You know what you have to do for
          us to stop.

INT. COMPOUND - LODGE - NIGHT

Mrs. Thompson sits in a rocking chair, reading a book
with the SEAL OF MALPHAS on the cover. Behind her, the
front door slowly opens. Ken slowly enters the room and
closes the door. Ken readies his hunting knife in his
hand. His machete still hangs from his side.

He watches her for a moment from behind as she reads.

                    KEN
          Hands up. Stand. Slowly.

Mrs. Thompson startles at the sound of his voice, then
puts the book down and slowly follows direction. She
turns around and faces Ken.

                                        (CONTINUED)

CONTINUED:

> **KEN**
> Mrs. Thompson?

> **MRS. THOMPSON**
> Oh, Mr. Williams! Thank God you're
> here! They have Chloe!

Ken studies her for a moment, not quite buying her act.

> **KEN**
> What are you doing here?

> **MRS. THOMPSON**
> They took me from my own home!
> They have your wife!

> **KEN**
> What?

> **MRS. THOMPSON**
> I saw Kathy! They have her too!

> **KEN**
> What do they want?

Mrs. Thompson shakes her head.

> **MRS. THOMPSON**
> Dear, I have no idea.

Ken lowers his knife.

> **KEN**
> Do you know where they're keeping
> Chloe?

Ken moves around the room, looking at things.

> **MRS. THOMPSON**
> I'm sorry, I don't. I haven't seen
> anything but this room.

Mrs. Thompson inches toward some knitting needles, while
Ken is looking around the room. Ken moves around the room
examining everything. She grabs a needle.

Ken's eyes fall on the book cover she was reading. It has
the demonic symbol of Malphas on the cover. Mrs. Thompson
starts to slowly move toward Ken with the knitting needle
behind her back.

> **KEN**
> The door wasn't locked.

CONTINUED: (2)

                    MRS. THOMPSON
          What?

                    KEN
          You said they locked you in this
          building.

He turns and looks at her.

                    KEN
          The door wasn't locked.

                    MRS. THOMPSON
          Oh? I suppose one of them left it
          unlocked...We should go!

                    KEN
          You never met my wife. You moved
          in a month after she left.

                    MRS. THOMPSON
          Well, I know from the pictures and
          flyers that Chloe showed me. That
          girl misses her mother something
          fierce, Mr. Williams.

Ken picks up the book, and tosses at her. It falls to the
floor, sigil up.

                    KEN
          ...And I suppose this is just some
          light reading? You're just
          curious?

Mrs. Thompson's demeanor changes. She smiles evilly.

                    MRS. THOMPSON
          My dear. I was just reading about
          how our Lord Malphas will feast on
          your soul!

Mrs. Thompson raises the needle above her head and
charges at Ken, SCREAMING. Ken grabs her arm, and forces
her to the ground. She drops the needle. He pins her on
the ground, face down.

                    KEN
          Where are they?

                    MRS. THOMPSON
          You're too late! It's begun!

                    KEN
          Shut up!

CONTINUED: (3)

Ken takes his hunting knife, and plunges it into the back of her skull. She goes limp.

The door bursts open and the bartender rushes in with a large knife.

                    BARTENDER
          Mom?! I heard screaming.

Ken looks up at the bartender. The bartender sees Mrs. Thompson.

                    BARTENDER
          Mom?!

                    KEN
          You gotta be fucking kidding me.

INT. CHURCH - NIGHT

Julian has Ava, his knife rests on her throat. Ava's lip is bleeding. Julian glares at Chloe. Jacob and Sean stand nearby and watch.

                    JULIAN
          Submit. Invite Malphas into your
          vessel, and we will spare your
          love, Ava.

Chloe looks at Ava.

                    CHLOE
          I won't do it.

                    AVA
          It's okay, Chloe. Don't do it.

Julian lightly drags his knife across Ava's cheek, drawing a tiny bit of blood. Ava screams.

                    JULIAN
          I'm losing my patience. Look at
          your mother, Chloe!

Chloe looks at Kathy's body.

                    JULIAN
          Is that what you want for Ava, as
          well? Or is it that you just don't
          love her enough?

                    CHLOE
          No! Leave her alone!

INT. COMPOUND - LODGE - NIGHT

Ken slams against the wall, the bartender charges at him
with his knife.

Ken dodges the thrust, and gets behind him. Ken grabs the
bartender's arm, and snaps his elbow over his knee. The
bartender SCREAMS, drops to the ground holding his elbow,
as the knife clatters to the ground.

                    KEN
          I've been going to your bar for
          about 9 months. Mrs. Thompson has
          been our neighbor for about the
          same time.

Ken squats down, and takes the bartender's injured arm.

                    BARTENDER
          Stop! What are you doing?

                    KEN
          Tell me what you have been doing.
          Why have you been watching us?

                    BARTENDER
          I can't.

Ken bends the arm. The bartender SCREAMS.

INT. CHURCH - NIGHT

Julian still has Ava. Chloe is still chained. Jacob and
and Sean are still watching. They hear the bartender
SCREAM in the distance.

                    JACOB
          What was that?

                    JULIAN
          Go check it out. Frank hasn't
          reported in lately. It could be
          our uninvited guest.

                    SEAN
          Consider it done.

                    JACOB
          Hail Malphas.

Jacob and Sean leave the room.

CONTINUED:

                         CHLOE
               You were talking about my dad,
               weren't you?

Julian glares at Chloe.

                         JULIAN
               Quiet! You are my child, not his!
               Don't get your hopes up for a
               happy reunion. If it is him, he'll
               be dead soon.

Julian slices Ava's forearm. Ava SCREAMS.

                         CHLOE
               Please! Stop!

                         JULIAN
               We have 22 hours to complete the
               ritual, child! I can torture poor
               Ava the entire day.

INT. COMPOUND - LODGE - NIGHT

The bartender SCREAMS again as Ken applies pressure.

                         BARTENDER
               Okay! We've been watching you and
               your daughter since your wife
               left.

                         KEN
               Why?

                         BARTENDER
               We've been waiting.

                         KEN
               For what?

The bartender looks up and smiles at Ken.

                         BARTENDER
               Tonight.

                         KEN
               October 5th.

                         BARTENDER
               That's right.

The bartender LAUGHS.

CONTINUED:

                    KEN
          What's so funny?

                    BARTENDER
          Did you not hear that scream?
          They're coming. You're fucked!

The bartender continues laughing. Ken grabs the bartender
and flings him forward onto the floor so he's face down.

                    BARTENDER
          Lord Malphas protect me!

Ken unsheathes his machete. Raises it, and swings it down
into the bartender's neck.

EXT. COMPOUND OUTSIDE LODGE - NIGHT

Jacob, and Sean slowly approach the lodge. The bodies of
Mrs. Thompson and the bartender decorate the front porch.
The bartender's head is in his lap.

                    SEAN
          No....

Jacob gets to the door, opens it, and looks in. He turns
back to Sean.

                    JACOB
          No one is here.

                    SEAN
          Where is he?

                    JACOB
          We have to find him before he
          causes more problems. We need to
          split up. Check every building.

INT. CHURCH - NIGHT

Julian still has Ava. Ava now has small cuts on her
forearm. Chloe is still chained.

                    JULIAN
          Tell me, Ava. How does it feel?

Ava looks up at Julian.

                    AVA
          How does what feel?

                                        (CONTINUED)

CONTINUED:

                    JULIAN
          How painful it must be to care for
          and love someone so deeply who
          doesn't feel the same for you.

Chloe sits up at attention.

                    CHLOE
          Don't listen to him, Ava!
               (to Julian)
          Shut your mouth!

Julian waves her off.

                    JULIAN
          Words. Just words. Ava, love is
          action. Love is sacrifice. I have
          been cutting you, and Chloe has
          done nothing. She can save you.

Chloe stands up and hurries to the edge of her chain.

                    CHLOE
          Shut! Up!

Julian chuckles.

                    JULIAN
          Look at her, Ava. She's all angry.
          Why would she get so mad, if what
          I'm saying isn't true?

Ava looks at Chloe.

                    JULIAN
          Poor Ava. We've been watching you
          all for almost a year now. You
          have been there for Chloe through
          everything. You're love for her is
          clear to us.

                    CHLOE
          Stop talking! Don't listen to him!

                    JULIAN
          Remember...love is action. Love is
          sacrifice, and you have sacrificed
          for Chloe, haven't you?

Ava looks up at Julian. Tear tracks streak her face.

                    CHLOE
          No, baby! Please.

CONTINUED: (2)

Ava looks at Chloe.

                    AVA
          Yes...I have sacrificed for her.
          I've put my life on hold to
          support her.

                    JULIAN
          Of course you have. Chloe and her
          missing mom have consumed your
          life for almost a year. And what
          has Chloe sacrificed for you? What
          actions has she take to show you
          that she loves you? She can save
          you, but refuses.

Julian punches Ava in the gut. Ava falls to her knees.

                    CHLOE
          No!

Julian slaps Ava across the face, sending her to the
floor. Julian paces back and forth in front of Ava. Ava
bleeds and writhes in pain on the floor.

                    JULIAN
          She has done nothing to show you
          love. We know. We've been
          watching.

Chloe stands.

                    CHLOE
          I know what you're doing!

Julian walks up to Chloe.

                    JULIAN
          Do you?

                    CHLOE
          You're trying to guilt me into
          sacrificing myself to Malphas for
          her. It's not going to work!

Julian turns back to Ava.

                    JULIAN
          Ava! Did you hear that? She
          doesn't even feel guilty about it!
                    (MORE)

CONTINUED: (3)

                    JULIAN (CONT'D)
          She has been perfectly happy to
          accept your love and support for
          nearly a year, giving nothing
          back, and doesn't feel an ounce of
          guilt about it.

Julian stomps on Ava's stomach. Ava cries out.

                    CHLOE
          Stop it!

                    JULIAN
          I can stomp on you, cut you, beat
          you, and Chloe doesn't care.

                    CHLOE
          That's not true!

EXT. COMPOUND - BEHIND LODGE - NIGHT

Sean cautiously walks along the building. He peeks around
a corner. No one can be seen. With his knife out in front
of him, he walks forward.

He slowly peeks around the corner of the building. No one
can be seen. He turns to walk away, and walks right into
Ken.

Ken quickly grabs Sean by the mouth to keep him from
yelling out and slams him against the wall. Sean's eyes
are wide. Ken recognizes him.

                    KEN
          Jesus. How many of you bastards
          have been spying on us?

Ken pulls the mailman off the door, moves behind him, and
snaps the Sean's neck.

INT. CHURCH - NIGHT

Ava looks up at Julian, and stands, bleeding and broken,
in defiance.

                    AVA
          No. I know she loves me. I can see
          it in her eyes.

Chloe gasps in relief.

                    CHLOE
          Oh, thank God!

                                        (CONTINUED)

CONTINUED:

Julian looks at her, and smiles.

                    JULIAN
          God? No. I'm afraid not. There is
          only Malphas here, and he's losing
          his patience.

Julian backhands Ava, sending her back into the wall. She
crumples to the ground.

                    CHLOE
          No!

Julian violently kicks and stomps on her.

                    CHLOE
          Please!

Julian turns back and screams at Chloe.

                    JULIAN
          She is going to die, unless you
          save her.

Ava weakly pulls herself to her hands and knees. Julian
walks back over to her, and plunges his knife through her
hand. Ava SCREAMS! Julian wraps Ava's chain around her
neck and starts choking her with the chain. Ava chokes
and gasps for air.

                    CHLOE
          I can't do this anymore!

                    AVA (CHOKING)
          Don't...

                    CHLOE
          I love you, Ava! I love you so
          fucking much! I willingly invite
          Malphas into my vessel!

Julian releases the chain. Ava falls the ground and gasps
for air. Julian stands and smiles.

                    JULIAN
          That wasn't so bad, was it?

Chloe SCREAMS and doubles over as pain overcomes her
entire body.

EXT. COMPOUND - OUTSIDE CHURCH - NIGHT

Jacob slowly makes his way back to the church, searching
for Ken. Ken steps out of the shadows about 50 yards in
front of Jacob. Old west standoff, style.

                    KEN
          I bet you're not even a fucking
          lawyer.

                    JACOB
          It's astonishing how slow you are.
          You have been two steps behind
          since the start.

Ken walks in an arc. Jacob matches Ken's pace moving away
from him.

                    KEN
          By my count, I've killed 4 of you
          delusional bastards, and I'll kill
          every last one of you, until I get
          to my daughter.

Jacob laughs.

                    JACOB
          See, that's what I'm talking
          about. Two steps behind. She's not
          your daughter, and her real daddy
          is taking real good care her.

Ken stops following Jacob. Jacob stops his pace. He
smiles back at Ken through the flames.

                    JACOB
          It must be so discouraging to know
          you're no match for us. You are
          not even smart enough to realize
          that I have to be a real lawyer.
          All those documents on the cabin
          were authentic. Your wife did own
          the cabin.

                    KEN
          You lured us here.

                    JACOB
          Did I? You're the geniuses who
          came. Don't blame me for your
          mistakes.

Jacob chuckles.

                                        (CONTINUED)

CONTINUED:

                    JACOB
          So, now what, hero?

Ken's eyes narrow.

                    KEN
          Now, I kill you, save my daughter,
          and burn this place to the ground.

Jacob laughs.

Ken throws one of his smaller knives at Jacob. It hits
Jacob in the left eye, and sinks to the hilt. Jacob's
laugh turns into a sick wail.

INT. CHURCH - NIGHT

Ava sits against the wall, recovering. Chloe is writhing
on the floor in pain.

                    CHLOE
          What's happening?

                    JULIAN
          Oh...Did I forget to mention the
          excruciating pain? Once your body
          adjusts to the power of Malphas
          that is flooding you, we will move
          on to phase 3.

The door bursts open, and Ken enters with his machete in
hand. Everyone turns to see him. Chloe is still on the
floor in pain.

                    CHLOE
          Dad! You're alive!

                    KEN
          Chloe!

                    AVA
          Mr. Williams!

                    JULIAN
               (to Ken)
          I'm impressed. I assume they're
          all dead?

Ken nods.

                    JULIAN
          A pity. Well, you're too late. For
          both of them.

                                        (CONTINUED)

CONTINUED:

Julian motions to Kathy's body. Ken sees Kathy's body.

                    KEN
          No...

He rushes to her side.

                    KEN
          Baby?

He cradles her head in his hands. Julian creeps up behind
Ken with his knife.

                    CHLOE
          Dad! Behind you!

Julian plunges his dagger into Ken's right shoulder. Ken
screams and lashes out with his right arm, striking and
pushing Julian backward. The knife stays in Ken's
shoulder.

Ken stands and turns, seething with anger.

                    KEN
          That was your one shot, and you
          fucked it up.

Julian stumbles backward as Ken leaps at him. Ken grabs
Julian by the face, and slams him against the wall.

                    JULIAN
          You can't stop what's coming.

                    KEN
          Maybe not, but I can make damn
          sure you're not around to see it.

Chloe doubles over in pain again, and screams. Ken turns
and looks at her.

                    KEN
          Chloe, Are you okay?

                    AVA
          Something's wrong with her!

                    CHLOE
          Dad, it hurts!

Julian reaches up and grabs the hilt of the knife in
Ken's shoulder and twists the knife. Ken screams but
doesn't let go. He head-buts Julian in the face.

CONTINUED: (2)

Julian lets go of the knife as his nose starts bleeding.
With his free hand, Ken pulls out the knife in his
shoulder. Julian laughs at him.

                    JULIAN
          It's too late. He's here.

                    KEN
          Then I'll fucking kill him too.

Ken plunges the knife into Julian's forehead. Julian's
body starts convulsing as Ken continues to hold him
against the wall. Ken let's Julian fall to the ground.

Chloe cries in pain on the floor, watching Ken.

                    AVA
          Mr. Williams! Get us out of here!
          There's something wrong with
          Chloe, and I think there's still
          more of them!

Ken takes a deep breath. He checks Julian's body and
finds the keys for the chains.

Chloe cries out again in pain.

                    AVA
          Hurry! Let me out, and I'll guard
          the door while you help Chloe!

Ken gets to Ava. He uses the keys to unlock the chain.
Ava throws her arms around Ken. Ken looks at Ava.

                    KEN
          Jesus. What did they do to you?

                    AVA
          I'm fine. Now help Chloe!

Ken pulls out his machete from his side, and hands it to
Ava.

                    KEN
          Take this.

Ava nods

                    AVA
          Got it.

Chloe screams again. Ken turns and walks to Chloe's
chain. Chloe struggles to stand.

CONTINUED: (3)

He starts to unlock the chain, when the end of the
machete bursts out the middle of his chest. Blood
splatters on Chloe.

                    CHLOE
          Dad?!

Ken looks at Chloe, shocked. He looks down at the machete
blade, and falls to his knees, revealing Ava standing
behind him.

Ken tries to speak, but blood flows from his mouth in a
gurgle. Ava pulls the machete back out his back. She then
swings the machete, and decapitates Ken.

                    CHLOE
          Nooo!!!

Ken's head lands near Chloe. Ken's body falls over.

A wave of pain washes over Chloe. She falls down, looking
up at Ava, smiling evilly down at her. Chloe sees a young
very attractive MAN emerge from the shadows behind Ava
before she passes out and everything goes black.

INT. CHLOE'S ROOM - DAY

The room is sunny and bright. Chloe's eyes flutter open.
Ava is laying next to her in bed. Ava has a warm and
loving smile on her face.

                    AVA
          Hi, sleepy head.

Chloe smiles at her.

                    CHLOE
          Hi. What happened?

Ava reaches over and caresses her hair.

                    AVA
          You've been sleeping.

                    CHLOE
          I had the craziest dream.

                    AVA
          Oh yeah? Was I in it? I better be
          the girl of your dreams.

They giggle together.

                                        (CONTINUED)

CONTINUED:

                    AVA
          So what happened?

Chloe thinks for a minute.

                    CHLOE
          I can't remember.

Ava turns and mounts Chloe. Chloe squeals with surprise
and delight.

                    AVA
          It doesn't matter, babe.

Ava holds down Chloe's wrists. Chloe starts to get
concerned.

                    AVA/MALPHAS
          I have you now.

Ava laughs with Malphas' laugh. Chloe struggles against
Ava, but she has and iron grip.

                    CHLOE
          Ava, let me go! What's happening?

Ava now has demon eyes.

                    AVA/MALPHAS
          I'm not Ava. We have work to do,
          you and I.

Chloe stops struggling.

                    CHLOE
          Who are you?

                    AVA/MALPHAS
          I am the Raven. I am he who
          builds. I am the master of your
          vessel. I am Malphas.

Waves of pain hit Chloe again. She screams and struggles.

                    CHLOE
          What is that?

                    AVA/MALPHAS
          My power is flooding your vessel.

                    CHLOE
          What do you want?

CONTINUED: (2)

                    AVA/MALPHAS
          I have what I want. I have you.

                    CHLOE
          My dad...

                    AVA/MALPHAS
          Is burning with me! His flesh will
          forever boil and blister.

Ava roars with demon laughter. Chloe shakes her head.

                    CHLOE
          No!

                    AVA/MALPHAS
          Do you feel it yet? The power?

                    CHLOE
          All I feel is pain.

                    AVA/MALPHAS
          Just wait. You will begin to hear
          the thoughts of those around you.

                    CHLOE
          I can read minds?

                    AVA/MALPHAS
          And that's just the beginning.

A thought occurs to Chloe.

                    CHLOE
          You can't win! He's dead! Your
          most devoted! My dad killed him.
          He can't be the final sacrifice.

                    AVA/MALPHAS
          You're so adorable.

Ava forces a kiss. Chloe struggles against Ava.

                    CHLOE
          No!

Chloe pushes up against Ava, but she disappears, and
Chloe now finds herself in...

INT. CABIN - LIVING ROOM - DAY

Chloe sits up on the couch of the cabin. Kathy sits in an
arm chair.

                                        (CONTINUED)

CONTINUED:

                    CHLOE
          Mom?

                    KATHY
          My beautiful girl.

Chloe looks around the cabin.

                    CHLOE
          You kept this place from us?

Kathy nods.

                    KATHY
          I kept lots of things from you.

                    CHLOE
          Mom, I'm scared.

                    KATHY
          I know, but it's okay. I see now.

                    CHLOE
          What?

Kathy stands up and walks to the couch and sits next to
Chloe. Kathy smiles at her and bushes her hand through
Chloe's hair.

                    KATHY
          I was wrong to keep you from Him.

Blood starts to leak from Kathy's mouth.

                    CHLOE
          No, momma.

                    KATHY
          All this blood spilt, because I
          kept you from Him.

                    CHLOE
          Please...

                    KATHY
          I'm at peace now. He has embraced
          me in his power.

                    CHLOE
          Mom, I love you!

Kathy grabs Chloe's face, and looks into her eyes. Kathy
now has demon eyes.

                                        (CONTINUED)

CONTINUED: (2)

                    KATHY/MALPHAS
          You. Are. Mine!

INT. WILLIAMS' HOUSE - LIVING ROOM - DAY

Chloe jumps, and finds herself on an armchair in the
living room of her house. Ken is sitting on the couch,
surrounded by empty beer cans, and drinking one. He nods
at her.

                    KEN
          Hey kiddo.

                    CHLOE
          What's happening?

Ken takes a swig of beer, his eyes never leaving Chloe.

                    KEN
          His power is flooding your
          essence, but you're fighting.

                    CHLOE
          How do I stop it?

Ken shakes his head.

                    KEN
          You don't. He's too powerful.
                (Malphas' demon
                 voice)
          What could a meager pathetic meat
          suit like you do against him?

                    CHLOE
          No! Not you, too!

Ken stands and drops his bear can.

                    KEN/MALPHAS
          Everyone you love leaves you. I
          will never leave you. I am
          everyone you've ever cared about.
          I am everyone you've ever loved. I
          am your world now. There is only
          me. Now, wake up!

INT. CHURCH - NIGHT

Chloe starts awake. Chloe is still chained to the wall of
the church. The pain is gone.

                                        (CONTINUED)

CONTINUED:

She turns to her right to see MALPHAS, mid-20s, very
handsome, sitting on a pew watching her. No one else is
in the room.

                    CHLOE
          Who are you?

                    MALPHAS
          You know who I am.

                    CHLOE
          Malphas.

Malphas smiles.

                    MALPHAS
          That's right...and now, I'm you.
          I'm In your mind, heart, and soul.
          I know every thought you've ever
          had. I know you better than anyone
          ever has.

                    CHLOE
          You don't know shit.

                    MALPHAS
          I know what it's like to be left
          by the people you love. My father
          banished us, and labeled us evil,
          and demons.

Chloe takes a moment to process his words.

                    MALPHAS
          See? You understand. We questioned
          one thing. Why he needed all of
          you, when he had us. When Lucifer
          tried to show him his new creation
          wasn't perfect, he banished us.

                    CHLOE
          The Bible says you're evil.

Malphas laughs.

                    MALPHAS
          Of course it does. Some would
          argue, it also says you are.

Chloe looks away from him.

CONTINUED: (2)

                         MALPHAS
               It's okay. You're with me now. I
               will never leave you. We are going
               to do wonderful things together.

                         CHLOE
               What do you want?

                         MALPHAS
               I want you to know, it's not all
               going to be bad. See, I'm a
               builder. I'm going to rebuild this
               world into the utopia dad wanted
               it to be. When he sees it, he'll
               know.

                         CHLOE
               Know what?

                         MALPHAS
               That despite being banished, I
               still love him.

Malphas laughs.

                         MALPHAS
               Of course, What these poor loyal
               disciples don't know, is that I
               will have to destroy everything
               that is first, starting with them.

                         CHLOE
               You claim to not be evil, but you
               don't kill people if you're good.

                         MALPHAS
               No? Dang. Do the victims of Sodom,
               Gomorrah, and The Flood know that?

                         CHLOE
               It's....not the same.

                         MALPHAS
               You forget. I know you're
               thoughts. You're not fooling me.
               You don't buy that shit either.
               The pain should be gone now. My
               powers will start kicking in.

                         CHLOE
               Powers?

CONTINUED: (3)

                    MALPHAS
          I told you in your dream. We can
          read minds, as well as control the
          minds of others.

                    CHLOE
          Are you mind controlling me now?

                    MALPHAS
          No. The attraction and empathy you
          feel towards me is genuine.

The door opens, and Ava enters, flanked by two hooded
cultists. Ava's wounds have been bandaged. She doesn't
acknowledge Malphas. Chloe looks at Malphas, puzzled.

                    MALPHAS
          Oh, you're the only one who can
          see or hear me.

                    AVA
          Good. You're awake.

Ava turns to the cult member.

                    AVA
          Go get anyone who's left. It's
          time for the final sacrifice.

Malphas stands.

                    MALPHAS
          Time to finish this.

The cult member nods and rushes out the door. Chloe looks
at Ken's head on the ground.

                    CHLOE
          You killed my dad.

                    AVA
               (screaming)
          No! HE killed your dad. He Killed
          my family!! He was supposed to die
          at the cabin!

                    CHLOE
          We trusted you! How can you be
          with these people?

Ava starts pacing.

CONTINUED: (4)

                    AVA
          We have been waiting for you for
          so long.

                    AVA (V.O. - TELEPATHY)
          That bitch hid you.

                    CHLOE
          What?

                    MALPHAS
          Oh! I told you about that,
          remember? One of my powers.

                    AVA
          Your mom hid you from us. We lost
          so many years of his glory on
          earth.

                    MALPHAS
          She's right. This should have
          happened years ago.

                    AVA (V.O. - TELEPATHY)
          It was so satisfying watching her
          bleed into your bowl, Lord
          Malphas.

Malphas smiles.

                    CHLOE
          You're sick. Don't even think
          about my mom.

Ava is surprised.

                    AVA
          Ahh...Malphas' power is kicking
          in. You're starting to read minds.

The hooded cultist rushes back into the room.

                    CULTIST #1
          They're ready.

                    CHLOE
          Malphas is going to destroy all of
          you! He'll destroy everything!

                    MALPHAS
          Oh! Come on now, spoilers!

CONTINUED: (5)

                         AVA
              You lie! He has promised to build
              heaven on earth.

                         MALPHAS
              Well, eventually.

                         AVA
              It's finally time.

EXT. COMPOUND - CLEARING IN THE MIDDLE OF THE BUILDINGS -
NIGHT

Half a dozen CULTISTS in robes surround the clearing. A
bonfire is blazing. Chloe, tied up, stands before Ava.
Ava has the ceremonial dagger. Malphas stands close to
Chloe, away from the cultists.

                         AVA
              The time has come! Those of you
              who remain, be blessed! You will
              welcome our Lord Malphas to this
              earthly plane!

                         CULTISTS
              HAIL MALPHAS!

Chloe's eyes are wide with shock and fear. She scans her
surroundings, searching for a way out of her predicament.

                         MALPHAS
              Listen to them! 'Hail Malphas!'
              They're sheep. It's pathetic. When
              I get control of you, I'm going to
              enjoy slaughtering them all and
              feasting on their intestines.

Malphas sees Chloe looking at him with disgust.

                         MALPHAS
              Oh! Sorry, my demon was showing.

                         CHLOE
              Listen too me! Malphas doesn't
              care about you! He will kill you
              all as soon as he takes full
              control of my body!

Ava turns to address her cultists.

CONTINUED:

                    AVA
          Don't listen to her! She is
          desperate, and will say anything!
          Don't let her shake your faith!

Chloe focus on different cultists, reading their minds.

                    CULTIST #2 (V.O. - TELEPATHY)
          Hail Malphas!

                    CULTIST #3 (V.O. - TELEPATHY)
          I am yours, my Lord!

                    MALPHAS
          Nice try. What now?

                    CHLOE
          I will not die here.

                    MALPHAS
          Of course not. It's you and me
          together, forever.

                    CULTIST #4 (V.O. - TELEPATHY)
          What if she's right? This all
          suddenly seems crazy? What am I
          doing here?

Chloe's eyes go wide.

                    MALPHAS
          Oh! You got one! How exciting!
          Can't wait to see what happens!

Chloe makes eye contact with Cultist #4.

                    CHLOE
          You! Help me! Please!

Ava turns and looks at Cultist #4.

                    AVA
          Oh? Have you had a less than loyal
          thought?

                    CULTIST #4
          No, High Priestess. I am loyal to
          Malphas.

                    MALPHAS
                (O.S. In Chloe's
                mind)
          Ha! What a fucking liar. I think
          you just fucked our friend here.

                                        (CONTINUED)

CONTINUED: (2)

                    AVA
          Then you should have no problems
          dying for him.

Ava address the rest of the cultists.

                    AVA
          Purge this cancer from our
          numbers.

                    CULTIST #4
          No! I believe! I'm loyal!

The other cultists pull out blades from their robes, and
descend upon Cultist #4 as he screams and they stab him.
Chloe cries as she watches.

                    MALPHAS
          Look what you did. You killed that
          guy, not me. You can't be good,
          and kill people, right? By the
          way, did you consider Ken good?
          Because he killed a bunch of
          people tonight, all for you.

                    CHLOE
          Fuck you.

The cultist retake their previous places around Chloe and
Ava.

                    AVA
          Now. Let's finish this, shall we?
          It's time for the final sacrifice.

                    CHLOE
          Ava, please. Don't do this.

Ava smiles. She raises her dagger above her head, over
Chloe and starts to bring it down.

                    CHLOE
          STOP!

Ava stops mid swing, like something is stopping her from
finishing the swing. Ava is shocked, and struggles to
move her hand and blade down, but can't.

The cultist look around, counfused.

                    CHLOE
          What happened?

CONTINUED: (3)

                    AVA
          I can't move.

                    MALPHAS
          The mind control kicked in, but
          you didn't read her mind just
          before she swung, did you?

                    CHLOE
          Shut up!

Chloe turns to Cultist #1.

                    CHLOE
          Untie me.

Cultist #1 walks over, and starts to untie Chloe.

                    CULTIST #1
          Sorry, High Priestess. This isn't
          me, I can't control myself.

The bindings fall to the ground. Chloe turns to the group
of Cultists.

                    CHLOE
          Kill yourselves.

All the Cultists start screaming as they start stabbing
themselves and each other against their will.

                    MALPHAS
          Wow! And you call me the evil one!

                    AVA
          What have you done!?

When the last cultist falls and dies, Chloe turns to Ava,
who still has her hand and knife suspended in the air.

                    CHLOE
          It's over.

                    AVA
          This can't be it!

                    MALPHAS
          I can feel your dilemma. What to
          do with her?

                    CHLOE
          I don't know.

                                        (CONTINUED)

CONTINUED: (4)

                    AVA
          Who are you talking to?

                    MALPHAS
          Let's see...She lied to you. She
          manipulated you. She killed your
          father. All this death and
          destruction is her fault. What do
          you want to do with her?

                    CHLOE
          She broke my heart.

                    MALPHAS
          The bitch, but a part of you still
          loves her.

Tears well up in Chloe's eyes.

                    CHLOE
          Yes.

Tears start to trail down Chloe's face as she looks into
Ava's eyes. Chloe reaches out, and runs her fingers
through Ava's hair.

                    CHLOE
          I love you.

                    AVA
          Let me go! I HAVE TO FINISH IT!

                    CHLOE
          Stab yourself....in the heart,
          like you stabbed mine.

Ava's hand and knife immediately swing down, and she
plunges the knife deep into her own chest. She looks up
at Chloe with shock, then smiles.

Blood starts to stream out of her mouth.

                    AVA
          Gotcha.

                    CHLOE
          What?

                    MALPHAS
          Yeah...should have slowed down and
          read her mind. It's okay, you're
          new at this.

Ava collapses onto the ground.

                                        (CONTINUED)

CONTINUED: (5)

                    AVA (O.S. - TELEPATHY)
          I have fulfilled the final
          sacrifice...His most devoted....

Ava dies.

                    MALPHAS
          I'll see ya soon.

Malphas disappears. Chloe stands in the clearing over all
the bodies. All is quiet. She looks around.

                    CHLOE
          Malphas?

Silence.

The unnatural sound of a ROCKING CHAIR slowly rocking
back and forth is heard. Chloe follows the sound to...

INT. COMPOUND - LODGE - NIGHT

Chloe, in a trancelike state, follows the sound of the
rocking chair and comes to the chair that Mrs. Thompson
was sitting in earlier.

The chair slowly rocks back and forth by itself.

Chloe slowly walks up to it. She reaches her hand out to
the rocking chair. The chair rocks toward her, and stops
as if her hand is touching the chest of someone sitting
in it.

The chair is now still. Chloe drops her hand, and stares
at the chair for a few beats.

POV - CHLOE

We watch the empty rocking chair from Chloe's POV for a
few tense moments.

Suddenly, Malphas, in true demon form, materializes out
of thin air as he leaps toward the camera.

                                        ROLL CREDITS

INT. TIM'S TRUCK ON A ROAD IN THE WOODS - MORNING

Tim is driving his truck to the address that Ken sent.

                                        (CONTINUED)

CONTINUED:

                    TIM
          God, I hope I'm not too late.

After a moment of driving, he sees Chloe on the side of
the road, walking the direction that Tim drives from. Her
clothes are tattered. She's dirty and covered with blood.

                    TIM
          Chloe?

Tim pulls over as he passes her. She keeps walking. Tim
gets out.

EXT. ROAD IN WOODS - MORNING

Tim starts to follow Chloe.

                    TIM
          Chloe!?

Chloe keeps walking. Tim jogs to catch up.

                    TIM
          Chloe?! What happened!

Tim reaches her, and grabs her shoulder. She turns
around. She has demon eyes. One red and one black.

                                        CUT TO BLACK

TIM SCREAMS

                    THE END

CONTINUED:

www.ingramcontent.com/pod-product-compliance
Lightning Source LLC
Chambersburg PA
CBHW060956260726
48661CB00005B/1900